D1117447

Take a trip to NIGERIA

Keith Lye

General Editor

Henry Pluckrose

Franklin Watts

London   New York   Sydney   Toronto

Facts about Nigeria

Area:
923,768 sq. km. (356,688 sq. miles)

Population:
84,968,000 (United Nations estimate, 1983)

Capital:
Lagos (a new capital is being built at Abuja)

Largest cities:
Lagos (pop. 1,061,000);
Ibadan (847,000;
Ogbomosho (432,000);
Kano (399,000)

Official language:
English

Main religions:
Islam, Christianity, local religions

Major exports:
Oil, cocoa, palm kernels, tin, rubber

Currency:
Naira

Franklin Watts Limited
12a Golden Square
London W1

ISBN: UK Edition 0 86313 070 4
ISBN: US Edition 0 531 04742 3
© Franklin Watts Limited 1983

Typeset by Ace Filmsetting Ltd,
Frome, Somerset
Printed in Hong Kong

Text Editor: Brenda Williams
Maps: Tony Payne
Design: Mushroom Production
Stamps: Stanley Gibbons Limited
Photographs: J. Allan Cash; Zefa, 6, 16, 23, 31; Nigerian High Commission, 10, 15, 19, 21, 26, 28, 29, 30; Colorpix/Ron Carter, 4
Front Cover: J. Allan Cash
Back Cover: Zefa

Nigeria is in West Africa. It became
an independent country in 1960. In
1958, oil was found in the hot, wet
lowlands of the south. Money gained
from selling the oil abroad has been
used by the government to modernize
this tropical country.

The country's official name is the
Federal Republic of Nigeria. It is
ruled by a president. The National
Assembly is Nigeria's parliament.
It has two parts. One is housed in the
Senate building in Lagos. The other
is the House of Representatives.

Lagos became the capital city of
Nigeria in 1914. It is a busy port in
the south-west that came under
British rule in 1861. A new capital
city is now being built at Abuja in
central Nigeria.

More people live in Nigeria than in any other country in Africa. Ibadan is the second largest city and has many modern buildings. It is the capital of Oyo state. The country has 19 states. Each one has its own government.

The north of Nigeria is much drier
than the south, and many buildings
are made of dried mud. Kano, an
ancient city, is the capital of Kano
state. It is the largest city in northern
Nigeria.

This picture shows some stamps and money used in Nigeria. The main unit of currency is the naira, which is divided into 100 kobo.

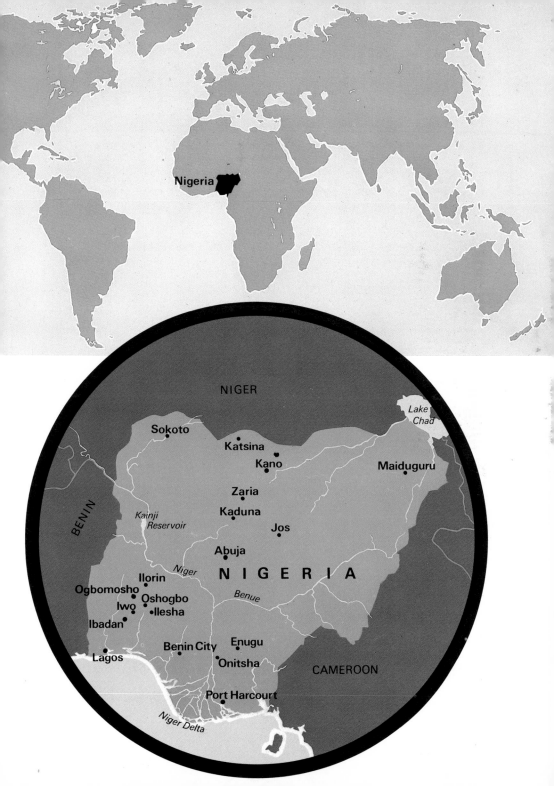

Nigeria

NIGER

Lake
Chad

Sokoto

Katsina

Kano

Maiduguru

Zaria

BENIN

Kainji
Reservoir

Kaduna

Jos

Abuja

Niger

N I G E R I A

Ilorin

Ogbomosho

Benue

Iwo

Oshogbo

Ilesha

Ibadan

Benin City

Enugu

Lagos

Onitsha

CAMEROON

Port Harcourt

Niger Delta

About 250 groups of people speaking different languages live in Nigeria. The horsemen in this picture are Hausa. They form the main group in northern Nigeria. These tall, elegant people are Muslims. Most of them are farmers.

Also in the north are the tall, slim
Fulani. Some roam the grassy
savanna with their herds of cattle.
The Muslim Fulani were once great
warriors. Some are still included
among the northern ruling classes.

The Yoruba are the chief people of the forested south-west. Many Yoruba are Christians or Muslims, but some follow their traditional religion. In the past, the Yoruba had powerful kingdoms and walled cities. Their art is famous.

The Ibo, or Igbo, live in the
south-east, mainly in villages built in
forest clearings. Most of them are
farmers or hard-working business-
men. The language used in business
and government is English. The
various parts of Nigeria have their
own languages, but English is
widely understood.

Islam is the chief religion of the north and also of many Yoruba in the south-west. Followers of Islam are called Muslims. Here they pray outside a mosque, a Muslim place of worship, at Zaria in northern Nigeria.

This Christian church is in Lagos.
Christianity is the most important
religion in the south. It was spread by
missionaries in the 19th century.

Local religions often have many powerful gods and spirits. Others have one High God. This shrine is in Oshogbo, in south-western Nigeria. It is used by followers of a local religion.

About half of Nigeria's people live in cities and towns. The rest live in villages and other settlements in the countryside. In the wet south, the mud walls of many homes are covered by thatched roofs.

Women in Nigeria enjoy wearing brightly patterned dresses when they go to market. Many Nigerians now wear western clothes. Others still keep their beautiful flowing robes.

These children are playing outside
their school. Primary schools are free
in Nigeria. But there are not enough
schools for all the children of
secondary school age.

Nigeria has 13 universities, but about 70 out of every 100 adults cannot read or write. A sewing class for adults is held in the open air in the northern state of Bauchi.

Palm kernels are pounded to a pulp so that the palm oil can be taken out. Palm kernels, cocoa and rubber are important crops grown in northern Nigeria for export.

Groundnuts, or peanuts, are sold at a market in northern Nigeria. Groundnuts and cotton are leading crops in the north. The north is also the main region for cattle and sheep-rearing. Goats are raised everywhere.

Yams are like sweet potatoes and are grown for food in southern Nigeria. Cassava, rice and plantains are also grown. In the north the climate is drier. Here millet, sorghum and rice are the chief foods.

Every year, a fishing festival is held at Argungu on a tributary of the Niger River near Sokoto in the north-west. At most times, the river has few fish. But on a certain day, fish come in great numbers. About 5,000 fishermen join in the festival.

Tin is mined in Plateau state and smelted in the town of Jos. Before oil was discovered, tin was Nigeria's most important mineral. It is still exported to other countries.

Nigeria has plenty of petroleum, as well as hydro-electricity from generators at dams on the rivers. So manufacturing industries are growing. One-fifth of the working people have jobs in industry. Here, television sets are assembled.

Fine bridges cross the mighty Niger River. This one is at Jebba in Kwara state. The Niger rises in distant Guinea and is Africa's third longest river. It enters the Gulf of Guinea through a huge, swampy delta.

This figure was made about 200 years ago in the kingdom of Benin in southern Nigeria. People have been making sculptures in Nigeria for over 2,800 years.

Sculpture is still important in Nigeria. Wood has always been popular for carving, but few of the old wooden sculptures are left now. Many have been eaten away by ants. But clay, metal and ivory pieces have survived.

Music, especially drumming, and dancing are among Nigeria's other important arts. Some kinds of western music, such as jazz and rock music, have their roots in the music of the slaves who were taken from Africa, including Nigeria.

Doctors and nurses are taught at the Training Hospital of the University of Ibadan. Their work is raising health standards in Nigeria. In 1960 most Nigerians could expect to live to 39 years of age. In 1980 they could expect to live to 49.

Index